My Body

My Stomach

by
Carol K.
Lindeen

Consulting Editor: Gail Saunders-Smith, PhD

Consultant: James R. Hubbard, MD
Fellow in the American Academy of Pediatrics
Iowa Medical Society, West Des Moines, Iowa

Capstone
press

Mankato, Minnesota

Pebble Books are published by Capstone Press,
151 Good Counsel Drive, P.O. Box 669, Mankato, Minnesota 56002.
www.capstonepress.com

072010
5843VMI

Library of Congress Cataloging-in-Publication Data
Lindeen, Carol, 1976–
    My stomach / by Carol K. Lindeen.
        p. cm.—(Pebble Books. My body)
        Summary: "Simple text and photographs describe the stomach, what it
does, and the process of digestion"—Provided by publisher.
        Includes bibliographical references and index.
        ISBN-13: 978-0-7368-6694-1 (hardcover)
        ISBN-10: 0-7368-6694-9 (hardcover)
        ISBN-13: 978-0-7368-7838-8 (softcover pbk.)
        ISBN-10: 0-7368-7838-6 (softcover pbk.)
        1. Stomach—Juvenile literature. 2. Digestion—Juvenile literature. I. Title.
II. Series.
QP151.L56 2007
612.3'2—dc22   2006027859

Note to Parents and Teachers

The My Body set supports national science standards related to anatomy and the basic structure and function of the human body. This book describes and illustrates the stomach. The photographs support early readers in understanding the text. The repetition of words and phrases helps early readers learn new words. This book also introduces early readers to subject-specific vocabulary words, which are defined in the Glossary section. Early readers may need assistance to read some words and to use the Table of Contents, Glossary, Read More, Internet Sites, and Index sections of the book.

Table of Contents

My Stomach

My stomach

is a body part

made of muscle.

It growls

when I'm hungry.

It gurgles after I eat.

My stomach
sometimes hurts
when I eat too much.
My belly sticks out.

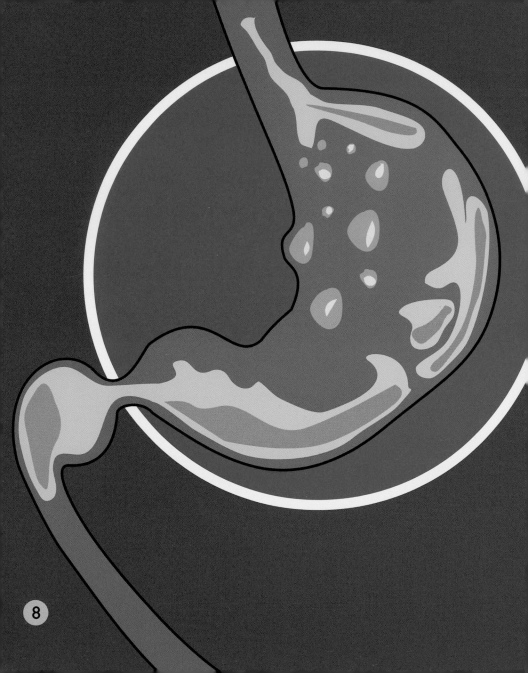

On the Inside

My stomach is stretchy.

My stomach gets
a little bigger
when it's filled with food.

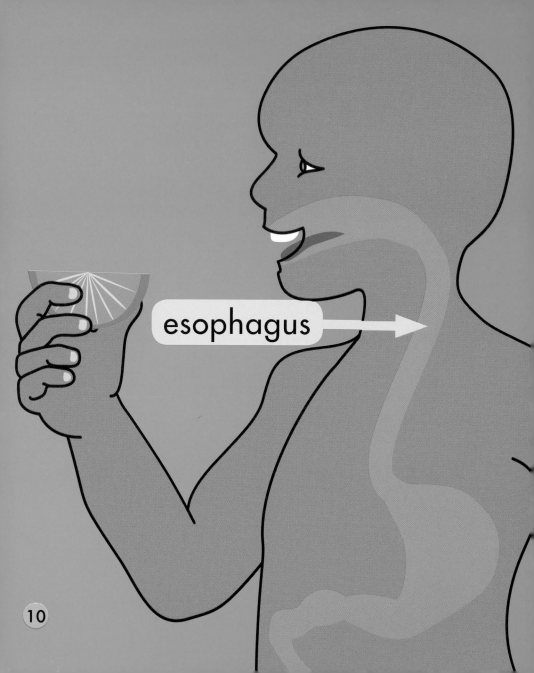

esophagus

My esophagus is
a long tube that goes
from my mouth
to my stomach.

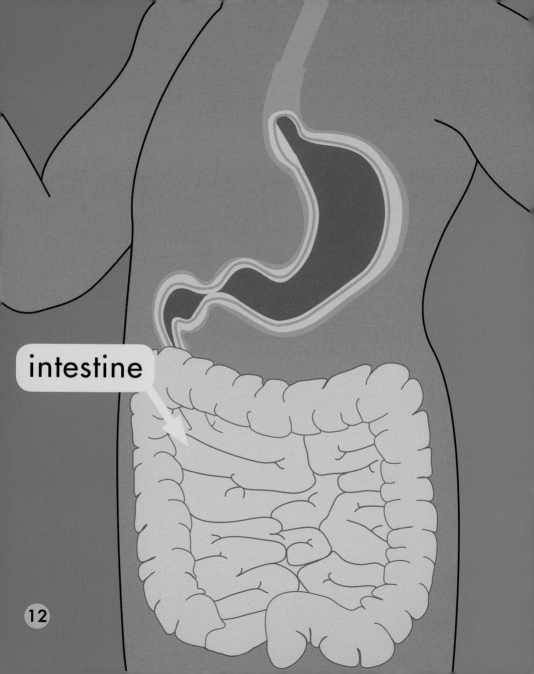

intestine

My intestine is
a long, winding tube.
It joins to the end
of my stomach.

My Stomach and My Body

When I eat,
food goes into
my stomach.

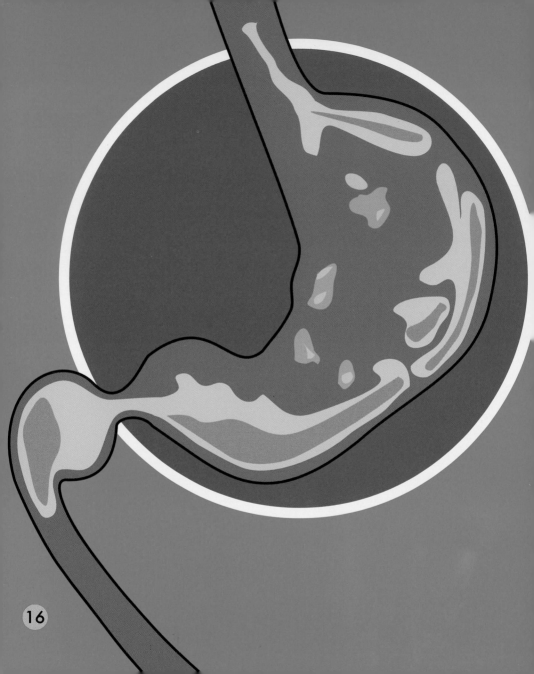

My stomach churns
and mashes food.
Juices and acid
in my stomach
help digest the food.

Food goes into my intestine. My body uses most of the food for energy. I get rid of the waste when I go to the bathroom.

Now it's time for a snack.
Soon my stomach
will be busy again
turning my food
into energy.

Glossary

acid—a strong liquid; acids in your stomach help break down food so your body can use the food for energy.

churn—to move roughly

digest—to break down food so it can be used by the body

esophagus—a long tube that carries food from the mouth to the stomach

growl—a low, deep noise

gurgle—a low, bubbling sound

intestine—a long, winding tube where food is digested; the body has a small intestine and a large intestine.

muscle—a body part that makes movement; your stomach and heart are muscles.

waste—food that the body doesn't need or use after it has been digested

Read More

Blevins, Wiley. *Where Does Your Food Go?* Rookie Read-About Health. New York: Children's Press, 2003.

Royston, Angela. *Why Do I Vomit?: And Other Questions about Digestion.* Body Matters. Chicago: Heinemann, 2003.

Internet Sites

FactHound offers a safe, fun way to find Internet sites related to this book. All of the sites on FactHound have been researched by our staff.

Here's how:

1. Visit *www.facthound.com*
2. Choose your grade level.
3. Type in this book ID **0736866949** for age-appropriate sites. You may also browse subjects by clicking on letters, or by clicking on pictures and words.
4. Click on the **Fetch It** button.

FactHound will fetch the best sites for you!

Index

Word Count: 144
Grade: 1
Early-Intervention Level: 16

Editorial Credits
Mari Schuh, editor; Bobbi J. Wyss, designer; Sandy D'Antonio, illustrator;
    Kelly Garvin, photo stylist

Photo Credits
Capstone Press/Karon Dubke, all